THE ULTIMATE

EMERIL LAGASSE

Power AirFryer 360 Plus™

COOKBOOK 2021

VEGETABLES & APPETIZERS

**The Most Comprehensive Guide
to Mastering Your Multicooker.**

*Steaming, Air Frying, Grilling and Searing Your Favorite
Meals in No Time!*

Book writing: Cookbook Academy Staff

Interior and Cover Designer: Laura Antonioli
Editor: Matt Smith
Production Manager: LP Business & Management LTD
Production Editor: Ash Rowling
Photography © 2020/2021: Janet Specter

COOKBOOK ACADEMY 2021 - by Ciro Russo

Given the great success of our publications, here are the links to other books written by us:

The Ultimate Ninja Foodi Cookbook 2021 - https://www.amazon.com/dp/B0914MSRH1
Pilot Kitchen - https://www.amazon.com/dp/B08TY8D66N

Table of Contents

Meatless Dishes • 51

Conclusion • 69

Introduction

In recent years, air fryers have become extremely popular.

They're popular with customers because they're lightweight, flexible, and capable of handling even the most difficult recipes. Since they cook in the same way, air fryers are often compared to convection ovens.

On top of air fryers, there is normally only one heating element, while convection ovens have three.

The Emeril Lagasse Power Air Fryer 360 has five heating elements and a 1500-watt engine.

It has 12 cooking presets, a memory feature, an extra-large capacity, and a brushed stainless-steel body that is both elegant and durable.

If you're thinking of planning to get an air fryer, wait a little longer and learn why an air fryer oven might be a better option for you.

We all want to eat more nutritious foods, but we don't want to give up our favorite foods in the process!

The Emeril Lagasse Power Airfryer 360 does just that: allows you to cook, bake, roast, and more delicious meals right on your kitchen countertop—without the use of oils, fats, or grease.

This powerful countertop oven, which uses a 360° whirlpool of superheated air to cook your food, can replace up to nine different kitchen cooking accessories, such as a convection oven, toaster oven, and other appliances, thus lowering the number of calories by almost every meal!

How Does the Emeril Lagasse Power Air Fryer 360 Work?

The hot air created by the heating elements is used to cook the food in air fryers. Convection fans circulate hot air to cook the food uniformly on all sides, similarly to convection ovens.

For best results, the 5 heating elements of the Emeril Lagasse Power Air Fryer 360 will be activated by the device depending on the cooking function chosen.

Air fried, toast, pizza, broil, bake, bagel, rotisserie, dehydrate, roast, reheat, warm, and slow cook are among the 12 presets. Between the top and bottom heating elements, there are four levels where you can position your tray, rack, or pan while cooking. For easy reference, the guide is also printed on the glass door.

Broiling and dehydrating are best done in the first position, closest to the top heating element. Toast, bagel, broil, air fry, dehydrate, and rotisserie functions are all available in the second position. The reheat, bake, roast, steam, pizza, and dehydrate functions are all found in the third position. Finally, the slow cook feature is found in the fourth position.

Programs and Functions

Air fry

The air fry feature will use the side heating elements for operation, with the air fry fans switched on. In the second location, position the crisper tray. It's better to use the baking tray and pizza rack just below the crisper tray while cooking foods with enough moisture or fat content that may drip during the cooking process.

Toast

To make those toasted brown colorations on both sides, the toast feature uses the top and bottom heating elements. From one to five, you can choose how dark your toast should be. It can toast six slices of loaf bread at once.

Bagel

The top and bottom heating elements are used in the bagel feature, while the air frying fans are switched off. You can fit up to six slices of bagels and choose the toast's darkness, just like with the toast feature. When this function is used, the pizza rack is moved to the second position.

Pizza

The top and bottom heating elements are used for the pizza function. The bottom heating unit crisps the dough, while the top heats the toppings and melts the cheese. During the cooking process, the air frying fans can be turned on.

Bake

The bake feature uses the top and bottom heating elements and allows you to switch on or off the air frying fans, it is ideal for baking pastries, cakes, and pies.

Broil

Broiling and melting cheeses over burgers, sandwiches, or fries is easy with the broil function. While the air frying fan is turned off, it uses the top heating element. To get the best results, the pizza rack should be positioned near the top heating part.

Rotisserie

The top and bottom heating components, as well as the revolving spit accessory, are used in the rotisserie function. Food turns brown and crispy on the outside while remaining sweet and juicy on the inside.

Slow cook

The top and bottom heating elements are used in the slow cook function. It works well with a Dutch oven, the baking dish with lid, or any other similar cooking pot for making tender pulled pork or beef brisket. The Power Air Fryer 360 can cook for up to 10 hours on "slow cooking" mode.

Roast

The roast feature is the better preset for cooking large cuts of meat since it equally cooks the meat on all sides. It also makes use of the heating elements on the top and bottom.

Dehydrate

Fruits, vegetables, and meat can all be dried using the dehydrate feature. To uniformly dry out the ingredients, it only uses the top heating element with the air frying fans switched on during the process.

Reheat

With the option to switch on the air frying fans, the reheat mechanism uses both the top and bottom heating components. It's perfect for reheating food that doesn't need to be seared.

Warm

With the air frying fans turned off, the warm mechanism uses the top and bottom heating elements. It's perfect for keeping food at a comfortable temperature until you're ready to serve it.

Benefits of Air Fryer Oven Cooking

Compact and versatile

Air fryer ovens, unlike traditional ovens, can comfortably fit on your kitchen countertop and be stored when not in use. They're adaptable and can do a variety of tasks in the kitchen.

Energy-efficient

Air fryer ovens heat up and cook 40% faster than bulky, regular ovens.

Rotisserie function

It allows you to easily cook a whole chicken, a leg of lamb, a big chunk of beef, or multiple kebabs. Some air fryer ovens have a rotisserie spit or drum, which makes roasting meat or other foods a breeze.

Bigger capacity than standard air fryers

The interior has several layers, allowing you to cook several foods at the same time. A whole chicken can be cooked in under an hour using just the Power Air Fryer 360.

Requires much less oil than traditional cookers

Air fryers use 70% less oil than regular deep fryers, making them a more cost-effective and healthier option.

Easy to clean

Stainless steel or aluminum are used in the majority of air fryer toast ovens. They are not only fashionable and beautiful, but they are also long-lasting and food-safe. The cooking chamber and removable parts are normally made of stainless steel or coated with a non-stick coating. The oven racks, air fry baskets, and other accessories are also dishwasher-safe.

Tips for Cooking Success

- Before using the appliance, make sure you complete the necessary initial steps.

- Foods with a smaller size will take less time to prepare. Cutting food into equal sizes will ensure easier and more even cooking, which will help you save time in the kitchen.

- A crispier texture can be achieved by spraying, misting, or gently brushing food with oil before cooking. Ensure that you don't add too much or it will get soggy.

- To achieve even cooking, turn or stir the food halfway through the cooking time.

- You can use the air fryer oven to make snack or pastry recipes that would normally be made in a conventional oven.

- Make sure the food isn't overcrowded. Allow some space between pans, particularly when cooking food with a coating or batter, to allow hot air to circulate and evenly cook the food.

- When making recipes that call for high temperatures, use oils with a high smoking point or that can withstand high temperatures. Avocado, peanut, and grapeseed oils are all good examples. The smoke point of olive oil is low. If you must use olive oil, use extra light olive oil, which has a higher smoke point and won't dry out the food until it finishes cooking.

- Do not put cooking trays or pans directly on the bottom heating elements, as this will prevent hot air from circulating properly and cooking the food.

- Oil and grease crumbs and drippings can cause smoke and burn. Place a baking tray lined with foil and parchment paper underneath the crisper tray or baking pan to avoid this.

Guidelines for Safety and Precautions

Reading the user manual is one of the first things you should do after getting your device. Not only will it advise you on the proper use, but it will also protect you from any accidents while using it.

For those of you who may have misplaced the instructions in the package (or for those who are simply a little distracted...) here are some of the guidelines to remember when using the Emeril Lagasse power air fryer.

DO

- This appliance is only meant to be used indoors.

- Only people with normal auditory, emotional, and physical abilities who have read and understood the manual should use the appliance.

- Keep out of wet areas and hot surfaces like stovetops.

- Place the air fryer oven on a counter or table that is stable, level, and heat-resistant.

- Leave at least five inches of clearance around the oven during service, as it can heat up and release steam.

- Once the oven is in operation, make sure there is no food protruding from it.

- When removing food from the oven, use oven mitts, gloves, or dish towels.

- Make sure the appliance is completely turned off before carefully unplugging it.

- After each use, unplug and clean the appliance.

- When the drip tray is halfway full, remove it and clean it.

- When removing any hot oil from the unit, use caution.

- Allow at least 30 minutes for the machine to cool fully after unplugging it.

DO NOT

- Use an extension cord with this appliance to prevent accidents.

- Use the unit without the drip tray installed.

- Place anything on top of the oven.

- Block the air vents, especially while the unit is turned on.

- Put flammable materials near or on top of the air fryer oven such as paper, plastic, curtains, towels, etc.

- Connect to an electrical outlet that is already used by other appliances as it may cause it to overload.

- Connect with an electrical outlet other than a 2-prong grounded 120V.

- Modify the plug or any part of the unit.

- Use accessories that are not recommended by the manufacturer.

- Clean parts with metal scouring pads and abrasive chemicals.

- Submerge the unit in water.

- Line the drip tray with foil.

- Use metal utensils or cutleries to prevent electric shock.

Follow the steps below when you are about to use the unit for the first time.

1. All packaging materials, labels, and stickers must be removed and properly disposed of before using your air fryer oven for the first time.

2. Use warm water and a mild detergent to clean the crisper tray, drip tray, pizza rack, baking pan, rotisserie spit, and rotisserie stand. Thoroughly dry the region.

3. With the aid of a moist cloth and a mild detergent, clean the exterior and interior. Make sure the fabric isn't too damp, as this could cause water to soak into some electrical components.

4. Connect the device to an outlet on the kitchen counter.

5. Burn off any protective coating or oil by preheating the oven for a few minutes. During this stage, it's common for some smoke to appear.

6. Turn the device off, unplug it, and allow it to cool fully. With a damp rag, wipe the interior and exterior once more.

Measurement Conversion

Often you'll come across a fantastic recipe that uses unfamiliar measurements, such as mL instead of cups. Conversion charts, whether metric, imperial, or gas label, come in handy in this case, assisting you in creating whatever recipe you want to try.

When cooking, it's a good idea to have a kitchen scale and a set of full measuring cups on hand to ensure that the ingredients are correctly measured.

Abbreviations for Cooking Measurements

When you're following a recipe, it's critical to know what the cooking abbreviations mean. When writing out recipes, many authors use shorthand, and if you don't know what it means, you may make a few mistakes.

Abbreviations for Imperial/Standard Measurement

lb = Pound
qt = Quart
tsp = Teaspoon
pt = Pint
Oz = Ounce
c = Cup
fl. Oz = Fluid ounce
gal = Gallon
Tbsp = Tablespoon (also TB, Tbl)

Abbreviations for Metric Measurement

kg = kilogram
g = grams
l = liter
mL = Milliliter

Liquid Ingredients vs. Dry Ingredients Measurement

When it comes to weighing, dry and liquid ingredients should be handled differently. Measuring cups and spoon sets are commonly used to measure dry ingredients, while liquid measuring cups are used to measure liquids. Exact measurements can be achieved by using the appropriate measuring instruments.

To get the most precise number when measuring dry ingredients, fill the cup to the brim and scrape the excess off the end. A liquid measuring cup cannot be used for this, which is why it should not be used. Although a liquid measuring cup will give you a more precise liquid measurement, when a recipe calls for small quantities of liquid, you will need to use measuring spoons instead.

These recommendations are particularly useful when preparing recipes that necessitate precise measurements.

Fluid Ounces vs Ounces

The difference between using ounces and fluid ounces comes down to the difference between liquid and dry ingredients. Weight is measured in ounces, while volume is measured in fluid ounces. Liquid ingredients are measured in fluid ounces, while dry ingredients are measured in ounces (by weight) (by volume). So just because a recipe calls for 8 ounces of flour doesn't mean you'll need 1 cup.

Most American recipes (using the standard/imperial system) would list dry ingredients in cups/tablespoons/etc. instead of ounces. Remember this when you're weighing your ingredients!

Basic Kitchen Conversions & Equivalents

In the kitchen, having a basic understanding of cooking measurements and conversions is important. When you're following a recipe, it's important to understand what everything means. You can't always find the darn tablespoon to measure out your ingredients, so you have to wing it... However, if you know that 1 tablespoon equals 3 teaspoons, you can weigh with confidence!

Simply follow these kitchen conversion charts, and you'll have them memorized in no time, just like your school's multiplication tables.

Conversion Chart for Dry Measurements.

3 teaspoons is equivalent to 1 tablespoon = 1/16 cup

6 teaspoons is equivalent to 2 tablespoons = ⅛ cup

12 teaspoons is equivalent to 4 tablespoons = ¼ cup

24 teaspoons is equivalent to 8 tablespoons = ½ cup

36 teaspoons is equivalent to 12 tablespoons = ¾ cup

48 teaspoons is equivalent to 16 tablespoons = 1 cup

Measurements Conversion Chart for Liquid

8 fluid ounces = 1 cup = ½ pint = ¼ quart

16 fluid ounces = 2 cups = 1 pint = ½ quart

32 fluid ounces = 4 cups = 2 pints = 1 quart = ¼ gallon

128 fluid ounces = 16 cups = 8 pints = 4 quarts = 1 gallon

Butter

1 cup butter = 2 sticks = 230 grams = 8 ounces = 8 tablespoons

Metric Cooking Measurement vs Standard Imperial Cooking Measurements

Metric to US Cooking Conversions

Oven Temperatures

- 120 c = 250 F
- 160 c = 320 F
- 180 c = 350 F
- 205 c = 400 F
- 220 c = 425 F

Baking in grams

- 1 cup heavy cream = 235 grams
- 1 cup sugar = 150 grams
- 1 cup powdered sugar = 160 grams
- 1 cup Flour = 140 grams

Volume

- 1 milliliter is equivalent to 1/5 teaspoon
- 5 ml is equivalent to 1 teaspoon
- 15 ml is equivalent to 1 tablespoon
- 240 ml is equivalent to 1 cup or 8 fluid ounces
- 1 liter is equivalent to 34 fl. ounces

Weight

- 1 gram = .035 ounces
- 100 grams = 3.5 ounces
- 500 grams = 1.1 pounds
- 1 kilogram = 35 ounces

US to Metric Cooking Conversions

- 1 pound = 454 grams
- 1 gallon (16 cups) = 3.8 liters
- 1 cup = 237 ml
- 1 tsp = 5 ml
- 1 tbsp = 15 ml
- 1 fl ounce = 30 ml
- 1 pint (2 cups) = 473 ml
- 1 quart (4 cups) = .95 liter
- 1 oz = 28 grams
- 1/5 tsp = 1 ml

What is 1 Cup Equivalent to?

Knowing what 1 cup equals is useful because, even if you don't have any kitchen measuring instruments, most people would have a 1 cup measurement. It can also be useful for cooking conversions while halving or doubling recipes. Just keep in mind that 1 cup equals these different measurements, so everything in this chart is equivalent!

- 1 cup = 8 fluid ounces
- 1 cup = 16 tablespoons
- 1 cup = 48 teaspoons
- 1 cup = ½ pint
- 1 cup = ¼ quart
- 1 cup = 1/16 gallon
- 1 cup = 240 ml

Baking Pan Conversions

(The cups denote the amount of batter that will fit into the pan.)

- 9-inch square pan = 8 cups
- 10-inch bundt pan = 12 cups
- 9 x 5 inch loaf pan = 8 cups
- 9-inch round cake pan = 12 cups
- 10-inch tube pan =16 cups
- 9-inch springform pan = 10 cups

Conversion of Common Baking Measurements to Ounces

- 1 cup unsifted powdered sugar = 4.4oz
- 1 cup all-purpose flour = 4.5oz
- 1 cup rolled oats = 3oz
- 1 large egg = 1.7oz
- 1 cup milk = 8oz

- 1 cup heavy cream = 8.4oz

- 1 cup granulated sugar = 7.1oz

- 1 cup packed brown sugar = 7.75oz

- 1 cup vegetable oil = 7.7oz

- 1 cup butter = 8oz

Ratings

In all of our cookbooks you'll find a grade of evaluation on each individual recipe called "Ratings".

The "Ratings" goes from 1 to 5 stars and it is determined by the complexity of the dish and the time you'll need to prepare it.

1 star will indicate a very quick and easy meal, while 5 stars will be a more complex recipe with higher preparation time needed.

We wanted to offer you this method of evaluating on every dish in order to make it even easier for you to choose the most suitable recipes according to your time availability.

Cookbook Academy Team

Vegetables and Side Dishes

Flavorful Potato Casserole

Preparation time
10 MINUTES

Cooking time
30 MINUTES

Servings
6

Ratings

Ingredients

2 lb potatoes, peel & shredded

1 1/2 cups sour cream

2 cups cheddar cheese, shredded

1/4 cup parsley, chopped

1/4 cup dill, chopped

1 small onion, minced

Pepper

Salt

Nutritional Info

Calories 328

Fat: 24.7 g

Carbohydrates: 15.5 g

Sugar: 1.2 g

Protein: 13 g

Cholesterol: 65 mg

Directions

1. Prepare a 9x13-inch baking pan by spraying it with cooking spray and setting it aside.

2. Add all ingredients into the mixing bowl and mix until well combined.

3. Pour mixture into the prepared baking pan.

4. Select bake mode. Set the temperature to 425 F and the timer for 30 minutes. Press start.

5. Let the air fryer preheat then insert the pizza rack into shelf position 5.

6. Place baking pan on the pizza rack and bake.

7. Serve and enjoy.

Butternut Squash Cubes

Preparation time
10 MINUTES

Cooking time
30 MINUTES

Servings
6

Ratings

Ingredients

2 lbs butternut squash, peel & cut into 1/2-inch cubes

2 tsp thyme, chopped

2 garlic cloves, crushed

2 tbsp maple syrup

2 tbsp olive oil

1 tsp salt

Nutritional Info

Calories 128

Fat: 4.9 g

Carbohydrates: 22.7 g

Sugar: 7.3 g

Protein: 1.6 g

Cholesterol: 0 mg

Directions

1. In a small bowl, whisk oil, thyme, garlic, maple syrup, and salt.

2. Add butternut squash into the mixing bowl. Pour oil mixture over butternut squash and toss well.

3. Spread butternut squash on a baking sheet.

4. Select bake mode. Set the oven to 400°F and timer to 30 minutes. Press start.

5. Let the air fryer preheat then insert the pizza rack into shelf position 5.

6. Place baking sheet on the pizza rack and bake.

7. Serve and enjoy.

Cheesy Baked Cabbage

Preparation time
10 MINUTES

Cooking time
10 MINUTES

Servings
6

Ratings

Ingredients

2 medium cabbage heads, cored & cut into 2-inch pieces

2 tbsp white sugar

3 tbsp flour

4 tbsp butter, melted

1 1/2 cups milk

1/2 tbsp white pepper

3/4 cup Swiss cheese, shredded

3/4 cup American cheese, shredded

1 tbsp salt

Nutritional Info

Calories 303

Fat: 16.6 g

Carbohydrates: 29.7 g

Sugar: 17.7 g

Protein: 12.7 g

Cholesterol 49 mg

Directions

1. Steam the cabbage. In a mixing bowl, mix cabbage, sugar, flour, butter, milk, and salt.

2. Transfer cabbage mixture into the baking dish. Sprinkle cheese on top.

3. Select bake mode. Set the temperature to 350 F and the timer for 10 minutes. Press start.

4. Let the air fryer preheat then insert the pizza rack into shelf position 5.

5. Place baking dish on the pizza rack and bake.

6. Serve and enjoy.

Spinach Zucchini Casserole

Preparation time
10 MINUTES

Cooking time
40 MINUTES

Servings
6

Ratings

Ingredients

2 egg whites
2 tsp garlic powder
1/2 tsp pepper
1/4 cup parmesan cheese, grated
2 small yellow squash, diced
1/2 cup breadcrumbs
1 tsp dried basil
2 small zucchini, diced
1/4 cup feta cheese, crumbled
3 cups baby spinach
1 tbsp olive oil
1/2 tsp kosher salt

Nutritional Info

Calories 109
Fat: 5.2 g
Carbohydrates: 10.9 g
Sugar: 2.6 g
Protein: 6.1 g
Cholesterol: 8 mg

Directions

1. Prepare a 9x13-inch casserole dish by spraying it with cooking spray and setting it aside.

2. In a medium-sized skillet, heat the oil.

3. Add zucchini, yellow squash, and spinach and cook until spinach is wilted about 5 minutes.

4. Transfer zucchini mixture into the mixing bowl. Add remaining ingredients and mix well.

5. Spread mixture into the prepared casserole dish.

6. Select bake mode. Set the oven to 400°F and timer to 30 minutes. Press start.

7. Let the air fryer preheat then insert the pizza rack into shelf position 5.

8. Place casserole dish on the pizza rack and bake.

9. Serve and enjoy.

Tomato Squash Zucchini Bake

Preparation time
10 MINUTES

Cooking time
30 MINUTES

Servings
6

Ratings

Ingredients

3 tomatoes, sliced

2 medium zucchinis, sliced

3/4 cup parmesan cheese, shredded

1 tbsp olive oil

2 yellow squash, sliced

Pepper

Salt

Nutritional Info

Calories 88

Fat: 5.1 g

Carbohydrates: 7.2 g

Sugar: 3.9 g

Protein: 5.7 g

Cholesterol: 8 mg

Directions

1. Prepare a 9x13-inch baking pan by spraying it with cooking spray and setting it aside.

2. Arrange sliced tomatoes, squash, and zucchinis alternately in the baking dish.

3. Drizzle with oil and season with pepper and salt.

4. Sprinkle parmesan cheese on top of vegetables.

5. Select bake mode. Set the temperature to 350 F and the timer for 30 minutes. Press start.

6. Let the air fryer preheat then insert the pizza rack into shelf position 5.

7. Place baking dish on the pizza rack and cook.

8. Serve and enjoy.

Baked Vegetables

Preparation time
10 MINUTES

Cooking time
35 MINUTES

Servings
4

Ratings

Ingredients

3 cups Brussels sprouts, cut in half

2 zucchini, cut in a thickness of 1/2-inch half circles

2 bell peppers, cut into 2-inch chunks

1 tsp thyme

8 oz mushrooms, cut in half

1 onion, cut into wedges

2 tbsp vinegar

1/4 cup olive oil

1/2 tsp salt

Nutritional Info

Calories 197

Fat: 13.4 g

Carbohydrates: 18.4 g

Sugar: 8.3 g

Protein: 6.1 g

Cholesterol: 0 mg

Directions

1. Prepare a baking sheet by lining it with parchment paper and setting it aside.

2. Add vegetables into the zip-lock bag.

3. Mix thyme, vinegar, oil, and salt and pour over vegetables.

4. Seal zip-lock bag and shake well and place it in the refrigerator for 1 hour.

5. Spread marinated vegetables on a baking sheet.

6. Select bake mode. Set the temperature knob to 375 F and the timer for 35 minutes. Press start.

7. Let the air fryer preheat then insert the pizza rack into shelf position 5.

8. Place baking sheet on the pizza rack and cook.

9. Serve and enjoy.

Cheesy Brussels Sprouts

 Preparation time
10 MINUTES

 **Cooking time**
25 MINUTES

 Servings
4

Ratings

Ingredients

15 oz Brussels sprouts, trimmed and cut in half

1/4 cup parmesan cheese, grated

3 garlic cloves, minced

1/4 cup breadcrumbs

3 tbsp olive oil

Pepper

Salt

Nutritional Info

Calories 184

Fat: 12.4 g

Carbohydrates: 15.5 g

Sugar: 2.7 g

Protein: 6.5 g

Cholesterol: 4 mg

Directions

1. Line baking sheet with parchment paper and set aside.

2. In a bowl, toss Brussels sprouts with breadcrumbs, cheese, garlic, oil, pepper, and salt until well coated.

3. Arrange Brussels sprouts on a baking sheet.

4. Select bake mode. Set the temperature knob to 390 F and the timer for 25 minutes. Press start.

5. Let the air fryer preheat then insert the pizza rack into shelf position 5.

6. Place baking sheet on the pizza rack and cook.

7. Serve and enjoy.

Healthy Zucchini Bake

Preparation time
10 MINUTES

Cooking time
45 MINUTES

Servings
6

Ratings

Ingredients

3 zucchini, grated

1/2 cup mozzarella cheese, shredded

1/2 cup feta cheese, crumbled

1/2 cup dill, chopped

3 eggs, lightly beaten

3 tbsp butter, melted

1/2 cup flour

Pepper

Salt

Nutritional Info

Calories 186

Fat: 11.5 g

Carbohydrates: 14.2 g

Sugar: 2.4 g

Protein: 8.4 g

Cholesterol: 109 mg

Directions

1. Prepare a 9-inch baking pan by spraying with cooking spray and set aside.

2. In a bowl, mix together zucchini, cheeses, dill, eggs, butter, pepper, flour, and salt.

3. Pour the zucchini mixture into the baking dish.

4. Select bake mode. Set the temperature to 350 F and the timer for 45 minutes. Press start.

5. Let the air fryer preheat then insert the pizza rack into shelf position 5.

6. Place baking dish on the pizza rack and cook.

7. Serve and enjoy.

Green Bean Casserole

Cooking time
25 MINUTES

Servings
4

Ingredients

1 lb green beans, cut into pieces and trimmed

1/4 cup parmesan cheese, shredded

1/4 cup olive oil

2 oz pecans, crushed

1 small onion, chopped

2 tbsp lemon zest

Nutritional Info

Calories 269

Fat: 24.1 g

Carbohydrates: 12.6 g

Sugar: 3 g

Protein: 5.7 g

Cholesterol: 4 mg

Directions

1. Add all ingredients into the bowl and toss well.

2. Spread green bean mixture into the baking dish.

3. Select bake mode. Set the temperature knob to 390 F and the timer for 25 minutes. Press start.

4. Let the air fryer preheat then insert the pizza rack into shelf position 5.

5. Place baking dish on the pizza rack and cook.

6. Serve and enjoy.

Eggplant Zucchini Casserole

Preparation time
10 MINUTES

Cooking time
35 MINUTES

Servings
6

Ratings

Ingredients

3 zucchini, sliced
4 tbsp basil, chopped
3 oz parmesan cheese, grated
1/4 cup parsley, chopped
1 cup cherry tomatoes, halved
1 medium eggplant, sliced
1 tbsp olive oil
3 garlic cloves, minced
1/4 tsp pepper
1/4 tsp salt

Nutritional Info

Calories 109
Fat: 5.8 g
Carbohydrates: 10.2 g
Sugar: 4.8 g
Protein: 7 g
Cholesterol: 10 mg

Directions

1. Prepare a baking pan by spraying with cooking spray and set aside.

2. Mix thoroughly all of the ingredients together in a big mixing bowl.

3. Pour eggplant mixture into the baking dish.

4. Select bake mode. Set the temperature to 350 F and the timer for 35 minutes. Press start.

5. Let the air fryer preheat then insert the pizza rack into shelf position 5.

6. Place baking dish on the pizza rack and cook.

7. Serve and enjoy.

Air Fryer Brussels Sprouts

Preparation time
10 MINUTES

Cooking time
14 MINUTES

Servings
2

Ratings

Ingredients

1/2 lb Brussels sprouts, halved and trimmed

Salt

1/2 tsp chili powder

Pepper

1/2 tbsp olive oil

1 tbsp chives, chopped

1/4 tsp cayenne

Nutritional Info

Calories 82

Fat: 4.1 g

Carbohydrates: 10.9 g

Sugar: 2.6 g

Protein: 4 g

Cholesterol: 0 mg

Directions

1. In a big container add all ingredients and toss well.

2. Spread Brussels sprouts in a crispier tray.

3. Place the drip tray below the bottom of the air fryer.

4. Insert the crispier tray into shelf position 4.

5. Select air fry mode. Set the temperature to 370 F and the timer for 14 minutes. Press start.

6. Serve and enjoy.

Rosemary Garlic Potatoes

Preparation time
10 MINUTES

Cooking time
15 MINUTES

Servings
4

Ratings

Ingredients

4 cups baby potatoes, cut into four pieces each

2 tsp dried rosemary, minced

3 tbsp olive oil

1/4 cup fresh parsley, chopped

1 tbsp garlic, minced

1 tbsp fresh lemon juice

Pepper

Salt

Nutritional Info

Calories 148

Fat: 10.8 g

Carbohydrates: 12.3 g

Sugar: 0.1 g

Protein: 2.6 g

Cholesterol: 0 mg

Directions

1. In a large bowl, add potatoes, garlic, rosemary, oil, pepper, and salt and toss well.

2. Spread potatoes in a crispier tray.

3. Place the drip tray below the bottom of the air fryer.

4. Insert the crispier tray into shelf position 4.

5. Select air fry mode. Set the temperature knob to 400 F and the timer for 15 minutes. Press start.

6. Transfer roasted potatoes in a bowl and toss with parsley and lemon juice.

7. Serve and enjoy.

Stuffed Peppers

Preparation time
10 MINUTES

Cooking time
25 MINUTES

Servings
6

Ratings

Ingredients

3 bell peppers, cut in half & remove seeds

1/4 cup feta cheese, crumbled

1/2 cup grape tomatoes, sliced

1/3 cup chickpeas, rinsed

1/2 tsp oregano

2 garlic cloves, minced

1 1/2 cups cooked quinoa

1/2 tsp salt

Nutritional Info

Calories 237

Fat: 4.8 g

Carbohydrates: 39.8 g

Sugar: 4.9 g

Protein: 9.8 g

Cholesterol: 6 mg

Directions

1. In a bowl, mix cooked quinoa, tomatoes, chickpeas, oregano, garlic, and salt.

2. Stuff quinoa mixture into the bell pepper halves and place in a baking dish.

3. Select bake mode. Set the temperature knob to 400 F and the timer for 25 minutes. Press start.

4. Let the air fryer preheat then insert the pizza rack into shelf position 5.

5. Place baking dish on the pizza rack and cook.

6. Top peppers with crumbled cheese and serve.

Air Fryer Garlic Mushrooms

Preparation time
10 MINUTES

Cooking time
15 MINUTES

Servings
4

Ratings

Ingredients

15 oz baby portobello mushrooms, halved

2 tbsp butter, melted

2 tsp coconut aminos

2 tsp garlic, minced

Nutritional Info

Calories 321

Fat: 5.8 g

Carbohydrates: 40.8 g

Sugar: 0 g

Protein: 40 g

Cholesterol: 15 mg

Directions

1. In a bowl, toss mushrooms with coconut aminos, garlic, and butter.

2. Add mushrooms to the crispier tray.

3. Place the drip tray below the bottom of the air fryer.

4. Insert the crispier tray into shelf position 4.

5. Select air fry mode. Set the temperature knob to 400 F and the timer for 15 minutes. Press start.

6. Serve and enjoy.

Lemon Cheese Asparagus

Preparation time
10 MINUTES

Cooking time
10 MINUTES

Servings
4

Ratings

Ingredients

1 lb asparagus, cut woody ends and trimmed

1 tbsp fresh lemon juice

1 tsp olive oil

1 oz feta cheese, crumbled

Pepper

Salt

Nutritional Info

Calories 52

Fat: 2.9 g

Carbohydrates: 4.8 g

Sugar: 2.5 g

Protein: 3.5 g

Cholesterol: 6 mg

Directions

1. Toss asparagus with lemon juice, olive oil, pepper, and salt in a bowl.

2. Add asparagus to a crispier tray.

3. Place the drip tray below the bottom of the air fryer.

4. Insert the crispier tray into shelf position 4.

5. Select air fry mode. Set the temperature knob to 400 F and the timer for 10 minutes. Press start.

6. Top with feta cheese and serve.

Tasty Green Beans with Onion

Preparation time

10 MINUTES

Cooking time

6 MINUTES

Servings

4

Ratings

Ingredients

1 lb green beans, trimmed

1/2 cup onion, sliced

2 tbsp olive oil

Pepper

Salt

Nutritional Info

Calories 101

Fat: 7.2 g

Carbohydrates: 9.5 g

Sugar: 2.2 g

Protein: 2.2 g

Cholesterol: 0 mg

Directions

1. In a bowl, toss green beans with oil, sliced onion, pepper, and salt.

2. Add green beans and onion to the crispier tray.

3. Place the drip tray below the bottom of the air fryer.

4. Insert the crispier tray into shelf position 4.

5. Select air fry mode. Set the temperature knob to 330 F and the timer for 6 minutes. Press start.

6. Serve and enjoy.

Curried Cauliflower Florets

Preparation time
10 MINUTES

Cooking time
10 MINUTES

Servings
4

Ratings

Ingredients

1 small cauliflower head, cut into florets

1 tbsp curry powder

2 tbsp olive oil

1/4 tsp salt

Nutritional Info

Calories 82

Fat: 7.3 g

Carbohydrates: 4.4 g

Sugar: 1.6 g

Protein: 1.5 g

Cholesterol: 0 mg

Directions

1. In a bowl, toss cauliflower florets with oil, curry powder, and salt.

2. Add cauliflower florets in a crispier tray.

3. Place the drip tray below the bottom of the air fryer.

4. Insert the crispier tray into shelf position 4.

5. Select air fry mode. Set the temperature knob to 350 F and the timer for 10 minutes. Press start.

6. Serve and enjoy.

Flavorful Cauliflower Florets

Preparation time
10 MINUTES

Cooking time
20 MINUTES

Servings
4

Ratings

Ingredients

5 cups cauliflower florets

6 garlic cloves, chopped

4 tablespoons olive oil

1/2 tsp cumin powder

1/2 tsp ground coriander

1/2 tsp salt

Nutritional Info

Calories 159

Fat: 14.2 g

Carbohydrates: 8.2 g

Sugar: 3.1 g

Protein: 2.8 g

Cholesterol: 0 mg

Directions

1. Add cauliflower florets and remaining ingredients into the large bowl and toss well.

2. Add cauliflower florets in a crispier tray.

3. Place the drip tray below the bottom of the air fryer.

4. Insert the crispier tray into shelf position 4.

5. Select air fry mode. Set the temperature knob to 400 F and the timer for 20 minutes. Press start.

6. Stir cauliflower florets halfway through.

7. Serve and enjoy.

Crispy Eggplant

Preparation time

10 MINUTES

Cooking time

20 MINUTES

Servings

4

Ratings

Ingredients

1 eggplant, cut into 1-inch pieces

1/2 tsp red pepper

1 tsp garlic powder

2 tbsp olive oil

1/2 tsp Italian seasoning

1 tsp paprika

Nutritional Info

Calories 99

Fat: 7.5 g

Carbohydrates: 8.7 g

Sugar: 4.5 g

Protein: 1.5 g

Cholesterol: 0 mg

Directions

1. Add eggplant and remaining ingredients into the bowl and toss well.

2. Add eggplant to the crispier tray.

3. Place the drip tray below the bottom of the air fryer.

4. Insert the crispier tray into shelf position 4.

5. Select air fry mode. Set the temperature knob to 375 F and the timer for 20 minutes. Press start.

6. Stir eggplant pieces halfway through.

7. Serve and enjoy.

Appetizer

Mozzarella Stuffed Mushrooms

 Preparation time
10 MINUTES

 **Cooking time**
10 MINUTES

 Servings
12

Ratings

Ingredients

1 cup tomato sauce

2 teaspoons fresh basil, chopped

12 large mushroom caps

1 cup mozzarella cheese, shredded

Nutritional Info

Calories: 112kcal

Carbs: 7.5g

Fat: 5.4g,

Protein: 10.5g

Directions

1. Mix the tomato sauce and basil leaves in a bowl.

2. Stuff the mushrooms with the mixture.

3. Sprinkle cheese on top.

4. Arrange mushroom caps inside the air fryer oven.

5. Select roast function.

6. Cook at 380 degrees F for 7 minutes.

Serving suggestion

Garnish with sliced basil leaves.

Tip

Do not rinse mushrooms. Instead, clean with a damp paper towel.

Tortilla Chips with Salsa

 Preparation time
10 MINUTES

 **Cooking time**
10 MINUTES

 Servings
6

Ratings

Ingredients

10 tortillas
Cooking spray
Salt to taste
3 cups salsa

Nutritional Info

Calories: 338kcal
Carbs: 43g
Fat: 17.0g,
Protein: 5g

Directions

1. Spray both sides of tortillas with oil.
2. Sprinkle with salt.
3. Slice into wedges.
4. Place the wedges in the air crisper tray.
5. Choose air fry option.
6. Cook at 350 degrees F for 4 minutes.
7. Flip and cook for another 3 minutes.
8. Serve with salsa.

Serving suggestion

Sprinkle with a little salt before serving.

Tip

Drain on a plate lined with paper towels.

Baked Ricotta with Herbs

Preparation time
10 MINUTES

Cooking time
10 MINUTES

Servings
8 TO 10

Ratings

Ingredients

30 oz. ricotta

4 teaspoons rosemary, chopped

4 eggs, beaten

1 tablespoon lemon zest

6 tablespoons Parmesan cheese

Salt and pepper to taste

Nutritional Info

Calories: 177.2kcal

Carbs: 5.8g

Fat: 10.1g,

Protein: 15.1g

Directions

1. Combine all the ingredients in a bowl.

2. Spread mixture into a small baking pan.

3. Set the air fryer oven to air fry.

4. For 10 minutes cook at 380 degrees F.

Serving suggestion

Sprinkle with a little pepper before serving.

Tip

Stop cooking when the edges turn brown.

Roasted Goat Cheese and Tomato Tarts

Preparation time
15 MINUTES

Cooking time
5 MINUTES

Servings
8

Ratings

Ingredients

1 tablespoon honey

1 teaspoon dried Italian seasoning

1/2 cup goat cheese, crumbled

1 pack crescent rounds, sliced into 8 rounds

2 tomatoes, sliced

2 tablespoons olive oil

Nutritional Info

Calories: 198.4kcal

Carbs: 16.2g

Fat: 12.6g,

Protein: 4.3g

Directions

1. In a bowl, mix honey, Italian seasoning and goat cheese.

2. Press the dough to form a flat circle.

3. Top the dough rounds with the honey mixture.

4. Put tomato slices on top.

5. Drizzle with olive oil.

6. Place these inside the air fryer oven.

7. Set the air fryer oven to roast.

8. For 5 minutes cook at 350 degrees F.

Serving suggestion

Sprinkle with pepper.

Tip

You can also use cream cheese for this recipe.

Chicken Nachos

Preparation time
15 MINUTES

Cooking time
5 MINUTES

Servings
4

Ratings

Ingredients

2 cups tortilla chips

1/2 cup chicken, cooked and shredded

1/2 cup black beans, rinsed and drained

1 jalapeno, sliced

1/2 cup fresh cheese, grated

1/2 cup cheddar cheese, shredded

Directions

1. Spread the tortillas chips in a baking pan.

2. Sprinkle the chicken, beans, jalapeno and cheeses on top.

3. Set the pan inside the air fryer oven.

4. Choose bake setting.

5. Cook at 350 degrees F for 3 to 5 minutes or until cheese has melted.

Nutritional Info

Calories: 399.3kcal

Carbs: 12.9g

Fat: 11.2g,

Protein: 59.1g

Serving suggestion

Serve with guacamole, lime wedges, sour cream and salsa.

Tip

You can also top nachos with chopped tomatoes.

Baked Potato Rounds

Preparation time
10 MINUTES

Cooking time
20 MINUTES

Servings
8

Ratings

Ingredients

2 potatoes, sliced into ½ inch thick rounds

Cooking spray

Salt and pepper to taste

1 cup sour cream

1 cup cheddar cheese, shredded

Nutritional Info

Calories: 160kcal

Carbs: 21g

Fat: 8g,

Protein: 2g

Directions

1. Spray potato rounds with oil.
2. Sprinkle with salt and pepper.
3. Add the potato rounds to the air crisper tray.
4. Select air fry setting.
5. Cook at 370 degrees F for 15 minutes, flipping once.
6. Let cool.
7. Top with sour cream and cheddar cheese.
8. Put these back to the air fryer oven.
9. Choose bake setting.
10. Bake at 350 degrees F for 3 minutes or until cheese has melted.

Serving suggestion

Sprinkle with dried herbs.

Tip

Use Russet potatoes for this recipe.

Bacon Wrapped Asparagus

 Preparation time
5 MINUTES

 **Cooking time**
10 MINUTES

 Servings
8

Ratings

Ingredients

1 lb. asparagus, trimmed
6 slices bacon

Nutritional Info

Calories: 109.6kcal
Carbs: 3.7g
Fat: 8g,
Protein: 6.6g

Directions

1. Wrap a couple of asparagus with bacon slices.

2. Organize in an air crisper tray in a single layer.

3. Set your air fryer oven to air fry.

4. For 10 minutes cook at 380 degrees F.

Tip

Before air frying, you can also sprinkle with maple syrup.STOP

Italian Olives

Preparation time

10 MINUTES

Cooking time

5 MINUTES

Servings

8

Ratings

Ingredients

2 cups green olives, pitted

2 cups black olives, pitted

2 tablespoons olive oil

2 cloves garlic, minced

½ teaspoon dried fennel seeds

½ teaspoon dried oregano

Pinch red pepper flakes

Salt and pepper to taste

Nutritional Info

Calories: 113kcal

Carbs: 0g

Fat: 0g,

Protein: 13g

Directions

1. Toss all the ingredients in a bowl.

2. Mix well.

3. Spread the olives in the air crisper tray.

4. Choose air fry setting.

5. Set temperature to 300 degrees F.

6. Cook for 5 minutes.

Serving suggestion

Serve immediately.

Tip

You can also use garlic powder instead of minced garlic.

Mini Lemon Crab Cakes

Preparation time
45 MINUTES

Cooking time
MINUTES

Servings
12

Ratings

Ingredients

24 oz. crab meat

3 green onions, chopped

3 tablespoons lemon juice

3 teaspoons lemon zest

6 tablespoons breadcrumbs

6 tablespoons mayonnaise

Nutritional Info

Calories: 24kcal

Carbs: 3g

Fat: 0g,

Protein: 2g

Directions

1. Combine all the ingredients in a bowl.

2. Shape into 24 small patties.

3. Refrigerate for 30 minutes.

4. Add the mini crab cakes to the air crisper tray.

5. Set your air fryer oven to air fry.

6. Cook at 370 degrees F for 5 minutes per side or until golden and crispy.

Serving suggestion

Garnish with half lemon slices.

Tip

You can also add fish flakes to the mixture.

Bacon Wrapped Dates

 Preparation time
5 MINUTES

 **Cooking time**
10 MINUTES

 Servings
12

Ratings

Ingredients

12 slices bacon

24 dates, pitted

Nutritional Info

Calories: 49.6kcal

Carbs: 6.3g

Fat: 2.3g,

Protein: 1.6g

Directions

1. Slice the bacon in half.

2. Wrap each date with a bacon slice.

3. Organize in a single layer in the air crisper tray.

4. Choose air fry setting.

5. Cook at 400 degrees F for 7 to 8 minutes.

Serving suggestion

Insert toothpick before serving.

Tip

You can also dip in balsamic vinegar before air frying.

Pizza Chips

Preparation time
15 MINUTES

Cooking time
MINUTES

Servings
12

Ratings

Ingredients

12 cheddar cheese slices, sliced into 4 smaller pieces

12 pepperoni slices, chopped

2 tablespoons dried oregano

Nutritional Info

Calories: 160kcal

Carbs: 14g

Fat: 10g,

Protein: 2g

Directions

1. Top the cheese slices with pepperoni and oregano.

2. Place these in the air crisper tray.

3. Choose air fry setting in your air fryer oven.

4. For 5 minutes cook at 350 degrees F.

Serving suggestion

Let cool to harden before serving.

Tip

You can also use a cracker and top it with the cheese.

Mini Clam Patties

Preparation time
10 MINUTES

Cooking time
5 MINUTES

Servings
8

Ratings

Ingredients

2 lb. clam meat, chopped
1 onion, minced
1 teaspoon garlic powder
2 stalks green onion, chopped
1/4 cup breadcrumbs
1 egg, beaten
Cooking spray

Nutritional Info

Calories: 1260kcal
Carbs: 112.6g
Fat: 55.6g,
Protein: 72.9g

Directions

1. Combine all the ingredients in a bowl.

2. Shape into 16 small patties.

3. Spray with oil.

4. Transfer patties to the air crisper tray.

5. Set your air fryer oven to air fry.

6. For 5 minutes cook at 350 degrees F per side or until golden and crispy.

Serving suggestion

Serve with sweet chili sauce.

Tip

You can also add fish flakes to the mixture.

Cheese Chips

 Preparation time
10 MINUTES

 **Cooking time**
5 MINUTES

 Servings
12

Ratings

Ingredients

12 cheddar slices, sliced into 4 pieces
Cooking spray

Nutritional Info

Calories: 456kcal
Carbs: 3.7g
Fat: 30g,
Protein: 41.6g

Directions

1. Spray cheese slices with oil.

2. Organize in a single layer in the air crisper tray.

3. Choose air fry setting.

4. For 5 minutes cook at 350 degrees F, turning once.

Serving suggestion

Sprinkle with dried Italian herbs.

Tip

You can Keep for up to 3 days in an airtight jar.

Mushrooms with Bacon and Cheese

 Preparation time
15 MINUTES

 **Cooking time**
MINUTES

 Servings
12

Ratings

Ingredients

3 tablespoons butter, melted

8 oz. cream cheese

8 strips bacon, cooked and chopped

Salt and pepper to taste

24 mushrooms

Nutritional Info

Calories: 14.5kcal

Carbs: 0.6g

Fat: 0.5g,

Protein: 1.7g.

Directions

1. Combine butter, cream cheese, bacon, salt and pepper in a bowl.

2. Top mushrooms with the mixture.

3. Place the mushrooms inside the air fryer oven.

4. Set the air fryer oven to roast.

5. for 5 minutes cook at 350 degrees F.

Serving suggestion

Garnish with chopped chives.

Tip

Use baby bell mushrooms or button mushrooms for this recipe.

Cranberry Brie Bites

Preparation time
10 MINUTES

Cooking time
7 MINUTES

Servings
12

Ratings

Ingredients

24 wonton wrappers

8 oz. brie cheese

2 cups cranberry sauce

Nutritional Info

Calories: 47.7kcal

Carbs: 8.5g

Fat: 1.5g,

Protein: 0.2g.

Directions

1. Line your muffin pan with wonton wrappers.

2. Place the muffin pan inside the air fryer oven.

3. Choose air fry setting.

4. For 3 minutes cook at 300 degrees F.

5. Top the wonton cups with cheese.

6. Place it back to the oven.

7. Select bake function.

8. Bake for 3 minutes or until cheese has melted.

9. Top with cranberry sauce and serve.

Serving suggestion

Garnish with cranberry slices.

Tip

You can also use other melty cheese.

Bacon Wrapped Cracker

 Preparation time
5 MINUTES

 **Cooking time**
5 MINUTES

 Servings
12

Ratings

Ingredients

12 crackers

12 slices bacon

1/4 cup Parmesan cheese, grated

Nutritional Info

Calories: 190kcal

Carbs: 23g

Fat: 9g,

Protein: 3g.

Directions

1. Wrap crackers with bacon slices.

2. Sprinkle with Parmesan cheese.

3. Place in the air crisper tray.

4. Choose air fry setting.

5. For 5 minutes cook at 350 degrees F per side or until bacon is crispy.

Serving suggestion

Serve with sweet chili sauce.

Tip

Do not overcrowd the air crisper tray.

Bruschetta

Preparation time
15 MINUTES

Cooking time
5 MINUTES

Servings
12

Ratings

Ingredients

4 tomatoes, chopped

1/4 cup fresh basil leaves, diced

1/4 cup Parmesan cheese, shredded

1 clove garlic, minced

1 tablespoon balsamic vinegar

1 teaspoon olive oil

Salt and pepper to taste

1 loaf French bread, sliced

Cooking spray

Nutritional Info

Calories: 67.1kcal

Carbs: 4.9g

Fat: 5.5g,

Protein: 0.7g.

Directions

1. In a bowl, incorporate all the ingredients except French bread.

2. Top the bread slices with the mixture.

3. Spray the bread with oil.

4. Organize in a single layer in the air crisper tray.

5. Choose toast or air fry setting.

6. For 2 to 3 minutes cook at 250 degrees F.

Serving suggestion

Sprinkle with pepper.

Tip

You can also use Italian bread for this recipe.

Pita Chips

Preparation time
6 MINUTES

Cooking time
4 MINUTES

Servings
8

Ratings

Ingredients

6 pita breads
4 tablespoons olive oil
2 teaspoons dried oregano
Pinch salt

Nutritional Info

Calories: 140kcal
Carbs: 18g
Fat: 6g,
Protein: 3g.

Directions

1. Slice pita bread into wedges.

2. Brush each side with olive oil.

3. Sprinkle with oregano and salt.

4. Organize in a single layer in the air crisper tray.

5. Set your air fryer oven to air fry.

6. Cook at 350 degrees F for 1 to 2 minutes per side.

Serving suggestion

Serve with ranch dip or French onion dip.

Tip

You can also season pita chips with Italian herbs.

Meatless Dishes

Sriracha Cauliflower Stir Fry

Preparation time
5 MINUTES

Cooking time
30 MINUTES

Servings
4

Ratings

Ingredients

1 head cauliflower, cut into florets

1 tablespoon Sriracha

1-1/2 tablespoons tamari or gluten free tamari

3/4 cup onion white, thinly sliced

5 cloves garlic, minced

1 tablespoon rice vinegar

2 tablespoons olive oil

1/2 teaspoon coconut sugar

Directions

1. Combine all the ingredients in a bowl.

2. Place the mixture in the air fryer.

3. Set the oven in air fry mode.

4. Cook at 350°F for 30 minutes, shaking the pot every 10 minutes.

Serving suggestion

Garnish with scallions.

Tip

You can use other hot sauces instead of sriracha.

Roasted Potatoes and Asparagus

Preparation time
10 MINUTES

Cooking time
5 MINUTES

Servings
4

Ratings

Ingredients

4 new potatoes, cut and cooked

1 lb. asparagus, chopped

1 teaspoon dried dill

2 stalks scallions, chopped

Salt and pepper to taste

Directions

1. Combine the asparagus, scallions, and olive oil in a small bowl.

2. Select the roast function and cook the mixture at 350°F for 5 minutes.

3. Combine the mixture with the potatoes in a large bowl.

4. Season with dill, salt, pepper, and olive oil.

Serving suggestion

Garnish with fresh parsley.

Tip

Drain the potatoes well.

Sweet Potato Casserole with Marshmallows

Preparation time
20 MINUTES

Cooking time
12 MINUTES

Servings
4

Ratings

Ingredients

Mini marshmallows

3 cups sweet potatoes, cooked and mashed

1/2 cup pecans, diced

1/2 cup brown sugar

1 teaspoon vanilla extract

1/3 cup melted butter

1 teaspoon ground cinnamon

Salt and pepper to taste

Directions

1. Combine all the ingredients, except for the mini marshmallows.

2. Set the mixture on a greased casserole dish.

3. Arrange the mini marshmallows on top.

4. Select the bake function on your air fryer oven.

5. Bake at 320°F for 10 to 12 minutes.

Serving suggestion

Serve immediately.

Tip

Use gluten-free marshmallows.

Grilled Vegetable Platter

Preparation time
15 MINUTES

Cooking time
15 MINUTES

Servings
6

Ratings

Ingredients

2 ears corn, quartered crosswise

8 oz. cremini mushrooms, halved

1 lb. asparagus, trimmed

1 lb. cherry tomatoes, stemmed

2 zucchinis, quartered lengthwise

3 tablespoons olive oil

Salt and pepper to taste

Directions

1. Grease the vegetables by brushing with olive oil.

2. Season with salt and pepper.

3. Set the oven in grill mode at medium heat.

4. Cook the vegetables, turning occasionally: mushrooms, asparagus, and mushrooms for about 3 or 4 minutes; corn and zucchini for 5 to 8 minutes.

5. Serve in a platter immediately.

Serving suggestion

Garnish with fresh basil leaves.

Tip

If available, season with Kosher salt and freshly ground black pepper.

Vegan Mini Lasagna

Preparation time
20 MINUTES

Cooking time
5 MINUTES

Servings
1

Ratings

Ingredients

2 lasagna noodles, halved and cooked

1/2 cup pasta sauce

1 cup baby spinach leaves, chopped

3 tablespoons zucchini

1 cup fresh basil leaves, chopped

1/4 cup tofu ricotta

Directions

1. Spread pasta sauce on a mini loaf pan.

2. Alternately layer the noodles with a mix of pasta sauce, spinach, zucchini, basil, and tofu ricotta.

3. Cover the loaf pan with aluminium foil.

4. Set the oven at 400°F on bake mode for 3 to 5 minutes.

Serving suggestion

Garnish with chopped parsley.

Tip

Use egg-free lasagna noodles.

Baked Zesty Tofu

Preparation time
30 MINUTES

Cooking time
10 MINUTES

Servings
4

Ratings

Ingredients

Sauce

2 tablespoons organic sugar

1/3 cup lemon juice

2 teaspoons arrowroot powder

1/2 cup water

1 teaspoon lemon zest

Tofu

1 tablespoon tamari

1 lb. extra-firm tofu, drained and pressed

1 tablespoon arrowroot powder

Directions

1. Incorporate all the sauce ingredients in a small bowl.

2. Coat the tofu with tamari, and then with arrowroot powder.

3. Set oven in bake function at 390°F.

4. Bake for 10 minutes, shaking halfway through.

5. Heat the tofu and sauce in a skillet over medium to high setting until the sauce thickens.

Serving suggestion

Serve with steamed rice and vegetables.

Tip

Use Meyer lemons to use less sugar.

Potato and Kale Nuggets

Preparation time
5 MINUTES

Cooking time
15 MINUTES

Servings
4

Ratings

Ingredients

1 teaspoon extra virgin olive oil
4 cups kale, chopped
1 clove garlic, minced
1/8 cup almond milk
2 cups potatoes, cooked
Salt and pepper to taste

Directions

1. Sauté the garlic and kale in oil for 2 or 3 minutes.

2. Mash the potato, adding milk, salt and pepper.

3. Combine the two mixtures, and then roll into 1-inch nuggets.

4. Cook on bake mode at 390°F for 12 to 15 minutes.

Serving suggestion

Serve with steamed rice or quinoa.

Tip

You may omit the olive oil, if desired.

Crispy BBQ Soy Curls

Preparation time
10 MINUTES

Cooking time
10 MINUTES

Servings
2

Ratings

Ingredients

1 cup soy curls
1 cup warm water
1 teaspoon vegetable broth
1/4 cup vegan barbecue sauce

Directions

1. Soak soy curls in warm water with vegetable broth for 10 minutes.

2. Drain and shred into a mixing bowl.

3. Cook on air fry setting at 400°F for 3 minutes.

4. Put back in mixing bowl and coat with barbecue sauce.

5. Air fry for another 5 minutes.

Serving suggestion

Serve with potato salad and collard greens.

Tip

In place of broth, you can use plain water.

Vegan Omelettes

Preparation time
10 MINUTES

Cooking time
8 MINUTES

Servings
3

Ratings

Ingredients

1/2 block of organic tofu
1/2 cup spinach, finely chopped
3 tablespoons nutritional yeast
1/2 teaspoon cumin
1/4 cup chickpea flour
1/2 teaspoon turmeric
1/4 teaspoon onion powder
1/4 teaspoon basil
1/4 teaspoon garlic powder
1 tablespoon apple cider vinegar
1/2 cup vegan cheese, grated
1 tablespoon water
Salt and pepper to taste

Directions

1. Puree all the ingredients in a processor, except for the spinach and cheese.

2. Combine the batter with spinach and cheese.

3. Make six omelettes into desired shape.

4. Cook on bake mode set at 370°F for 4 minutes on each side.

Serving suggestion

Serve in a sandwich.

Tip

Use a cookie cutter to shape your omelettes.

Cajun Fishless Filets with Pecan Crust

Preparation time
5 MINUTES

Cooking time
15 MINUTES

Servings
3

Ratings

Ingredients

3/4 cup water

1 teaspoon Cajun seasoning blend

3/4 cup pecans, minced

3 tablespoons flax seed, ground

1/4 cup plus 2 tablespoons cornmeal, finely ground

10.1 oz. Gardein Golden Fishless Filets

Directions

1. Make batter by combining all the ingredients except for the filets.

2. Coat the filets with the batter.

3. Cook on roast mode at 390°F for 10 minutes.

4. Flip and roast for another 3 to 5 minutes.

Serving suggestion

Serve with rice and hot sauce.

Tip

You can check if the center is piping hot—meaning it's cooked—by poking with a fork.

BBQ Tofu Wings

 **Preparation time**
15 MINUTES

 **Cooking time**
20 MINUTES

 Servings
4

Ratings

Ingredients

1 block extra firm tofu, cut in triangle wings

3/4 cup barbecue sauce

1/2 cup white wheat flour

1/4 cup cornstarch

Directions

1. Lightly brush the tofu with barbecue sauce.

2. Coat with cornstarch and flour.

3. Arrange on a lined baking sheet.

4. Cook using the bake setting at 350°F for 10 minutes.

5. Remove from air fryer and coat with sauce again.

6. Bake for another 10 minutes.

Serving suggestion

Top on a salad with a side of tahini dressing.

Tip

Use a rubber spatula when removing from air fryer to keep the tofu and coating intact.

Brussels Sprouts and Sweet Potatoes

Preparation time

15 MINUTES

Cooking time

20 MINUTES

Servings

4

Ratings

Ingredients

4 cups Brussels sprouts, sliced lengthwise

6 cups sweet potato, diced

2 tablespoons low-sodium soy sauce

2 teaspoons garlic powder

Directions

1. Season the veggies with garlic powder.

2. Set the air fryer oven to roast mode at 400°F.

3. Roast the Brussels sprouts for 5 minutes.

4. Roast the sweet potatoes for 15 minutes.

5. Season the veggies with soy sauce, and then cook for another 5 minutes.

Serving suggestion

Serve with quinoa and peanut butter sauce.

Tip

Also try with tahini sauce.

Bacon Tofu

Preparation time
10 MINUTES

Cooking time
20 MINUTES

Servings
4

Ratings

Ingredients

1 block tofu, pressed and sliced
1 tablespoon olive oil
1/4 cup soy sauce
1 tablespoon liquid smoke
3 tablespoons balsamic vinegar
1 teaspoon garlic powder

Directions

1. Incorporate all the ingredients in a small bowl, except for the tofu.

2. Marinate the tofu with the mixture for 30 minutes.

3. Use the air fry setting of your oven.

4. Air fry at 400°F for 18 to 22 minutes.

Serving suggestion

Serve with grains or in a sandwich.

Tip

You can dice the tofu for salads and soups.

Sticky Orange Tofu

Preparation time
30 MINUTES

Cooking time
10 MINUTES

Servings
4

Ratings

Ingredients

1 tablespoon tamari
1 tablespoon cornstarch
1 oz. extra-firm tofu, cubed

Sauce

1/3 cup orange juice
1 tablespoon pure maple syrup
2 teaspoons cornstarch
1/2 cup water
2 teaspoons cornstarch
1 teaspoon orange zest
1 teaspoon fresh ginger, minced
1 teaspoon fresh garlic, minced
1/4 teaspoon crushed red pepper flakes

Directions

1. Prepare the sauce by incorporating all the ingredients.

2. Coat the tofu with tamari, and then with cornstarch.

3. Use the air fry setting of your oven at 390°F.

4. Cook for 10 minutes, shaking halfway through.

Serving suggestion

Serve with steamed rice and vegetables.

Tip

You can also pair this with vegan noodles and fried rice.

Salted Broccoli with Lemon

Preparation time
5 MINUTES

Cooking time
15 MINUTES

Servings
4

Ratings

Ingredients

Salt and pepper to taste
1.1 teaspoon garlic powder
2 tablespoons olive oil
Fresh lemon wedges
1 lb. broccoli

Directions

1. Drizzle broccoli with olive oil.
2. Toss in salt, pepper, and garlic powder.
3. Set the oven on air fry mode at 380°F.
4. Air fry for 12 to 15 minutes.

Serving suggestion

Serve with lemon wedges.

Tip

Flip and shake for at least three times while cooking.

Cheesy Brussels Sprouts with Garlic

 Preparation time
35 MINUTES

 **Cooking time**
25 MINUTES

 Servings
4

Ratings

Directions

. Add all the ingredients together, except for the Parmesan cheese.

. Select the roast function on your air fryer oven.

. Roast Brussels sprouts for 20 minutes.

. Sprinkle cheese, and then roast for another 3 minutes.

rving suggestion

Serve warm.

Tip

You may vegan cheese instead of Parmesan cheese.

Quinoa Pilaf with Garlic Tofu

 Preparation time
10 MINUTES

 **Cooking time**
15 MINUTES

 Servings
4

Ratings

Ingredients

1 cup quinoa, cooked in vegetable broth

1 cup green peas, cooked

1 block extra-firm tofu, sliced and pressed

2 cloves garlic, minced

2 lemons, zested and juiced

Salt and pepper to taste

Directions

1. Make a marinade with garlic, lemon zest, lemon juice, salt, and pepper.

2. Marinate the tofu for 15 minutes.

3. Cook tofu on air fry setting at 370°F for 15 minutes.

4. Mix the quinoa pilaf, boiled green peas, and tofu.

Serving suggestion

You can serve warm or cold.

Tip

You can also try this with rice instead of quinoa.

Conclusion

Dear Reader,

I can tell you in all confidence that I have tested all the recipes above and have been satisfied not only with their excellent success but also with the performance of Emeril, without which I would not have achieved such results! That's why I have poured into this book all the experience and expertise accumulated during my culinary experiments, and that's why I am convinced I can help you solve many problems. At least in the kitchen!

;)

So go ahead and experiment with your Emeril Lagasse air fryer, and remember: your imagination is the first and most valuable ingredient in any recipe!

Ciro